PRINTHOUSE BOOKS PRESENTS

I0079515

RISEN

The accession and devolution of Yahweh Ben Yahweh

Miami's Urban Chronicles; Volume I

Thomas Barr Jr.

True Fiction

©Thomas Barr Jr.; 2015

PrintHouse Books, Atlanta, GA.

Published: 1-15-2016

www.PrintHouseBooks.com

VIP INK Publishing Group; Incorporated

Thomas Barr Jr.

Cover art designed by Beyond Graphics.

Editor: Cheryl Hinton

ISBN: 978-0-9970016-24

Library of Congress Cataloging-in-Publication Data
#2015956922

1. Urban Literature 2. True Fiction
2. Religion 4.Thomas Barr Jr. 5.Miami,
   Florida

Printed in the United States of America

This novel is dedicated to Lake City High School

class of 89, the Brown family, the Fulmore family,

the Butler family, the Barr family, The Wilson

family, the Cooper family, the Mitchell family and

Enid Oklahoma.

The growth of "Mega churches" has risen

considerably in the 21st century as compared to the

past. Miami's Urban Chronicles Volume I: Risen,

seeks to set forth a fictional biopic of the rise of

spiritual leader Yahweh Ben Yahweh of the Liberty

City based movement the Nation of Yahweh, "Ben

Yahweh's."

Chauncey Miller, the main character in the story

is determined to be a success. He uses his natural

skills of cultivating relationships and influence to

draw his followers. Despite his meager rural

southern background he dreams big and takes risks

head-on in realization of his goals. It is significant

in modern 21st century times that individuals take

control of their life's path. The urban youth

particularly need to realize by making deliberate

decisions concerning their life they can live their dreams.

Chauncey meets a mentor whom cultivates his ideology and sharpens his mediation skills in working with people. He harnesses his skills by working with the youth ministry of a local church. As he attends college he learns the basics of economics and administration in his courses. He understands education is just one tool that can help him along his path. Individuals must utilize opportunities as they present themselves along life's path. The main character seizes upon this truth and follows it down the rabbit hole in a manner of speaking.

In most communities the Church is a place of worship, fellowship, family, communal meetings and refuge. Individuals seek comfort in its walls and the main character leverages this in amassing followers. Modern successful pastors have PhD's and fancy seminary school training. The main character can be viewed as the progenitor to the modern "Mega church" system. He is of the conviction that god must call a person to preach which is a spiritual mission.

The main character takes this mission on as any other profession and is determined to be a success as a spiritual leader, messenger of god, as well as a successful business entrepreneur. The main character goes from city to city while growing his followership and refining his professional talents. In addition his studies have led to him evolving his religious convictions.

The story enthralls with the turmoil of power, beliefs, sex, control, and all the human pitfalls that too often affect successful professionals. In desiring success and wealth upon any career path it is important to maintain composure. Chauncey, although a spiritual leader, is in realization of this truth.

In paralleling the lifestyles of the larger community many individuals become disillusioned and pigeonhole themselves. Only in selflessness can individuals walk a blemish-less path. Particularly urban youth must learn the lesson in traversing modern life goal paths in reaching their dreams.

This chronicle wraps with Chauncey answering to the communal guidelines of this prescribed society. All must answer to the allegations of their

fellow community members and none is an

exception to this rule. In acquisition of success and

goal setting humility can be a lifesaver.

Table of Contents

PROLOGUE

An elderly man pulled a water hose over a thick hedge of bush and then doubled over as he grabbed his balls. He groaned loudly, the feeling of numbness flushed through his groin area which made his knees buckle. A lady ran over and led him to a chair that sat up under an old live oak tree in her yard. He was unsure how he would carry on his landscape business considering the condition of his health. His hedge equipment was scattered throughout the yard and he needed to finish loading the truck. He would catch his breath and finish the job he thought to himself.

The shade was a delight for the old gentlemen. He sat as the South Florida sun shone down on his silvery thick mane. A light wind blew and the white robe he wore flapped in the breeze. The lady returned with a glass of ice-cold water. The glass was cold to the touch as the old man grasped it and drank with long gulps. The lady stood and watched the old man; his Adams apple rose and fell as he downed the liquid. He handed over the empty glass; the ice clinked loudly because of the movement. Months earlier the old timer experienced a bone pain that resulted in a horrible pelvic fracture. He was out of work for a while and was determined to get things back rolling after his recovery.

As the lady took his glass she slipped a folded bill into the man's shirt pocket. The man rose gathered his equipment and was down the road in his truck. He pulled into a yard filled with Bald Cypress, Bottle Brush and Royal Poinciana floras.

This was home for the old man and he coveted the

work he put into it. He grabbed an old tattered book

of scriptures and positioned himself in a rocking

chair on his front porch. He read a while and

scribbled in the margins of the pages as he rocked

back and forth. He paused for a moment and

marveled at a Poinciana that was in bloom. The old

man was surrounded by life on his porch. He was

happy he had survived life in the 21st century. He

grimaced as he lost his bladder control and wet

himself.

***

CHAPTER 1 - The Early Years

Chauncey Miller was a Carolina native that grew up in the south and knew the hard work of the tobacco fields. Raised in a Christian household he was fascinated with the bible and studied religion with a fervor. Little did his contemporaries know that he would, one day, rise to the level of a spiritual leader commanding a multi-million dollar enterprise. They surely wouldn't realize that he was a megalomaniac capable of manipulating a band of killers.

It's a sunny afternoon in 1976 and Chauncey was on the corner of 125th Peachtree Street in Atlanta, Georgia. He had a stack of paper leaflets, as pedestrians approach he offered a flyer to a man dressed in a black suit. The man took the flyer and read it, mouthing the words soundlessly.

"Do you believe in god," asked the man in black.

"Surely I do," responded Chauncey sternly.

The man continued to look at the flyer; he wore iron-rimmed glasses and had shiny black shoes.

"I'm a history professor at the local community college and would like to have you join one of my focus group," he asked.

The man stood and looked Chauncey in the face awaiting an answer to his inquiry. Chauncey had not expected such an immediate attention to himself and paused in response noting the man's patient nature.

"I'm not sure what focus groups do but if you give me the address I'll check it out," said Chauncey.

The man pulled a business card from his blazer and handed it to Chauncey as pedestrians ushered pass them on the street. No one seemed to notice the exchange between the two men and was oblivious of them obstructing the walkway as they chatted.

"Don't worry you'll find out when you show," the man replied.

He placed the flyer Chauncey gave him in his coat and continued on his way. Chauncey looked down at the flyers he had been passing out for the street team company. He had been working for the company weekends and at afterhours bar locations. Exhausted he read it. It said; *let me tell you why the white man is the devil. Come hear CL*

Cayman speak truth to power at White Hall located

on Jackie Robinson Avenue.

Chauncey never took notice of the leaflets

he passed along to pedestrians and this one had a

very inquisitive message. He wondered about the

thoughts of the gentleman in which he had just met,

had the message affected him so profoundly? He

took the business card from his pocket looked at the

address and contemplated the location. He had seen

the address before on something he read at home

and could not recall it due to his momentary failing

memory.

The stack of leaflets sat on the sidewalk near

a lamppost. A gust of wind arose that blew some of

the top flyers into the street. The sudden barrage of

papers broke his thoughts and he scrambled to grab

them as people continued to bustle past.

"Get out the street," yelled a disgruntled

driver.

He blew his horn as he drove past and

Chauncey continued to pick up the flyers ignoring

the outburst. Chauncey had hardened his feelings to

ridicule and he believed his ability to project an icy

persona could ward off potential personal threats.

As a youth he had dealt with bullies, and

experienced being "singled out" for jokes among

friends in the neighborhood. He had developed this

ability while in grade school and used it throughout

his young adult life as he entered his college years.

He decided he would attend the focus group

the following day after his last class on campus and

find out more about the strange gentleman that
intrigued him on their meet.

***

Claude Donors, in his sixties, was a tall wiry
light-skinned complexioned man with green eyes
who did social research on religions in historical
contexts. He was an eccentric man with a direct
nature. Chauncey's curiosity of the gentleman had
led him to the campus upon the issued invitation.
Donor's secretary immediately stopped Chauncey at
the door as he entered Mr. Donor's university
office. "I'm sorry sir do you have an
appointment?" She inquired.

The young woman was very pretty and
Chauncey noticed that she had a curvy figure. He
could see that she was highly educated by the way
she addressed him. She was smartly dressed in a

business suit. She smelled of light perfume and

mints. Her hair was pinned up into a bun and she

sat positioned at her office desk. He quickly handed

over the business card given him and she looked at

the back of the card for a moment.

"Have a seat Dr. Donors will be with you in

a minute," said the young lady.

Chauncey took back the card he had given

the girl and looked on the back of it as she did his

curiosity peeked. *Let this man pass,* it said written

in a very legible hand written signature. He had not

noticed it the entire time he had possession of the

card and was surprised at himself for not realizing

that fact.

As he sat awaiting Dr. Donors he noticed

the office was cozy and decorated with plaques

along the light blue colored walls. The carpet

smelled freshly vacuumed, and it being in the late evening, there was not much pedestrian traffic. He noticed the young lady pick up the phone a number of times and she talked for just a few minutes on each instance. He assumed it was Donors and wondered if he made the right decision in coming. Just as the thought popped in his head Donors brushed by him.

"Let's go young man, we're late." He said.

Chauncey was out of his chair and behind Donors as he strode down the hallway taking giant steps to reach his desired location quickly.

"My focus group is designed to record the assumptions, thoughts, and impressions of religion on the average working class individual," he said as they walked.

"By the way what's your name?" he asked turning to look at Chauncey.

"Chauncey Miller," Chauncey replied.

"Well Mr. Miller you should find this to be very interesting," he said as they entered a room with about seven people sitting around a circular table. Upon introduction by the four males and three females it was noted two were teachers, one was a factory worker, two were students, one was a paramedic, and one was a shopkeeper. The questions posed to the group were designed to elicit discussion and the professor recorded all responses.

The first question posed was, "do you believe in god? Followed up with, "what do you think about religion?" All the participants believed in god but it was interesting to see their apparent ambiguity in the actual practice of religion. As the professor guided the group's discussion a light bulb went off in Chauncey's head. He had wondered throughout his life what his purpose was in this world. He had attended college and taken on various odd jobs to support himself in the city. He'd bounced around in search of a career interest to no avail. He was articulate and well regarded for his ability to persuade others. In observing the professor's research he saw a need and an opportunity that could possibly be exploited. He decided from that instance he wanted to know more about the professor and the purpose for his work.

The session ended after about an hour of discussion and all the participants departed leaving Chauncey alone with the professor in the room. As the professor put the finishing touches on the session notes Chauncey broke the silence which

permeated the room after the last departed guest.

"What made you want to pursue this type of

study sir," he inquired. Chauncey set up in the chair

he was seated in to hear the response. He did not

intend to disturb Donors but he was very interested

in knowing what motivated him. The motivation of

a man can be a key factor in determining character

and Chauncey needed to determine the character of

this enigmatic man.

Donors paused and stopped his scribbling

for a moment. He placed his pen on the desk and

rocked back in his chair. He seemed to be in deep

thought as he contemplated the question. He

cleared his throat and spoke in a controlled manner.

His voice came across clear and his words were

contemplative.

"This issue was a lingering concern of mines while I myself was a fraught youth in school," He replied. Donors went on to explain his upbringing and the basis of his decision to go to college. As he spoke Chauncey could see the passion he had for the issue and the man impressed him.

"I'm interested in your work and would like to offer you my assistance," he said. Chauncey knew he could be a benefit to Donors in his study and he also hoped to get more insight into the mechanics of the theory.

"I thought this would interest you more than passing out flyers for fanatics," replied the professor. Chauncey listened intently to the words the professor spoke. He was excited about the chance to work with a university professor. In those few seconds he imagined the knowledge he could learn from this man and his work. He had been waiting for this type of opportunity for a long time.

"Welcome to the fold my son," exclaimed Donors.

CHAPTER 2 - Indoctrination

Chauncey considered himself a leader of men and felt disillusioned with the secondary education process. He majored in economics at the local college but many graduates he knew were unemployed upon graduating. They additionally had acquired hefty student loans to repay once creditors were notified that they were out of school. The entire system is a rip off thought Chauncey to himself as he walked across the campus on his way to class. He was always good with numbers and was phenomenal in math. In school he was often elected as treasurer in class organizations. His experience in these activities stoked his thirst for leading others and managing money for project developments.

He pushed open a large door leading to the entrance of the classroom hallway. A few students mingled around before going into the room for the seminar. Chauncey entered the classroom and slid into his seat at the back of the room. The lecture had already started and he doodled on a notepad as the professor lectured on the relationship of spirituality in the 21st century. The professor made note of the inclinations of individuals to seek out enlightenment in the coming years by way of religion. Chauncey often thought deep on this concept and speculated how he could capitalize on this prospect. Many hardliners in religion are of the opinion that religious leaders are "called upon" by the most high. Chauncey would seek to utilize the ministerial role to penetrate into the masses for acquiring power and control. He thought deep on the process Dr. Donors used in getting detailed knowledge on the sociological functions of people in regard to religion. He would align himself with the doctor and learn all he could about pastoral leadership.

"Remember a seven page report is due next week for discussion," replied the professor.

The students filed out the classroom and Chauncey had missed the entire lecture engulfed in his thoughts. He exited the classroom full of hope at his new endeavor to become a preacher.

***

Chauncey rented a room from a retired military captain who was the landlord of an old flophouse not too far from campus. The place a bit run down was in need of major repairs, and much-needed upgrades. The rent was cheap but the condition of the living quarters were not fit for a refugee. Four males maintained rooms in the beat up old house and the old captain lived on the first floor of the two-story monstrosity. As he lay on the bed in his room he heard a knock at the door.

"Miller, rent due," said the voice on the other side of the door.

Chauncey dreaded when the old captain made his door-to-door runs for collecting rent and he surely was not ready for him this week.

"I'll see you this weekend," he yelled still reclined on his bed.

"You said that last week," replied the old captain.

"This weekend, Saturday," replied Chauncey.

• • •

"It's Saturday or you'll be kicking cans," said the old captain.

He shuffled down the hall continuing his knocking on doors and Chauncey sighed relief to hear him move on from his doorway. He knew that he needed money and he had to develop some skill that could ensure him a sustainable way to eat. He mentally assessed what his best qualities were in himself. He knew he was a people person and he especially enjoyed teaching others. He thought maybe he could be some type of teacher but outside of being a professor they were not paid their worth. He did enjoy reading ancient documents and doing research for various topics. He knew his skills and interests would need to be used on a scholarly basis for whatever direction he chose career wise. He thought about the studies Dr. Donors was conducting on religion and surmised it could be a

key in advancing his interests.

***

Being adept at research and having a

voracious appetite for reading Chauncey acquired

books on sermons. He pilfered the college library

for old recorded tapes of Muslim, Christian and

Catholic leaders. He tailored his studies in school

to psychology and studies of the social inclinations

of human in the social sciences field. He studies

now gave him vigor in learning and renewed his

since of hope in himself. He felt compelled to the

Christian Preachers mode of leadership because he

grew up with that as a young child. However, he

deeply admired the Muslim model in the ability to

quickly recruit and motivate black youth.

"You curious about religion, huh?" asked the clerk as he checked out a couple of books for Chauncey.

"Just doing research," he responded cautiously.

"The Flag of Islam by Author Elijah Muhammad," stated the clerk aloud as he stamped the book.

"Brother, I'm kind of in a rush," replied Chauncey glancing behind him.

"Listen," said the clerk as he leaned over the counter. "There's an NOI branch meeting on campus in Thompson Hall later tonight."

"What's NOI?" replied Chauncey.

"Nation of Islam man," said the clerk with irritation. "307, check it out, it might do you some good," he stated as he shoved the books over the counter in Chauncey's direction.

Chauncey figured that attending the meeting would give him direct insight into the infrastructure of how the operation functioned. He was not aware of the rhetoric taught by the NOI and was interested in what would be presented to those in attendance.

***

Chauncey entered the entrance of the dormitory and looked door to door searching for the numbers 307. The dormitory was remarkably quiet and few people wandered the hallways of the building. He soon stepped in front of a door with 307 in bold printed numbers and knocked three times. A male opened the door dressed in all black he looked at Chauncey and then glanced down the hall.

"Come in my brother," he said.

Chauncey recognized the person as the clerk from the library and followed him inside down a narrow hallway. A group of men sat on the floor of a spacious room and one man was standing giving instructions from a book. Chauncey was directed to a space on the floor and he sat trying to understand what was occurring in the room.

"Don't worry we're just starting," said the clerk. "They're just wrapping up old business."

The man standing was dressed in a black suit and wore a bow tie. His shirt appeared starched crisp white and he was neatly dressed. He was clean cut and articulate as he spoke to those seated around him.

"Islam is the only religion that addresses the needs and wants of the black man in America," said the neatly dressed man.

The man went on to discuss the slave trade and how religion was used to control those enslaved. He went on to discuss how this country turns a blind eye to injustices done to black people and gave examples of the double standards of the law. He quoted statistical numbers and gave references of the facts he presented to the group. Chauncey was impressed with the presentation and with the men that attended. At the end of the presentation the attendees were invited to attend service at the temple the following week and Chauncey decided to join them

* * *

CHAPTER 3 - Recruitment

The temple was located near Tech Square on
5th and Spring Street. It was a simple building with
no elaborate decorations, as you would see on
Catholic and Mega Christian churches. There was a
cone shaped speaker on the door and various
sermons were played for passers-by on the street.
Chauncey joined the NOI and was one of its chief
followers in community development work and
black empowerment activities. He often worked the
street corners doing grassroots recruitment for the
organization. He felt freedom voicing anger and
discontent of the system against black folks in the
community.

"I'm tired out here pushing this rhetoric and black folks not listening," said one of the young recruiter ministers.

He had a hand full of flyers under his arm and he flopped down on a nearby bench on the street corner. It was a sunny day and Chauncey had passed out most of the materials he had on teachings of the NOI. He disliked hearing sob stories of why others refused to do things that they were tasked to do. He mentally blocked the ramblings of his associate and thought about owning his own house of worship. He visualized himself leading a faithful flock and having access to riches.

"Brother Chauncey did you hear me?" asked the young man.

"Yeah but if you don't pass the rest of your flyers off like I did the minister is going to have your head," replied Chauncey in a stern voice.

The young man shrugged and lifted himself from the seated position and stood in front of the bench. People continued to straggle past as he attempted to tell them of future sermons in the temple. Some people pushed past him and mumbled something incomprehensible as they passed. A few stopped long enough to hear what was said and took a flyer.

***

Chauncey appreciated the time spent doing grass root recruiting on the streets and he truly believed it helped craft his oratorical skills. His knowledge of the teachings of the NOI was far more advanced than others because of his many hours of study at the campus library. He had also

noted the references in the book indexes' of those at

the temple. The minister of the temple recognized

the genius Chauncey exuded and promoted him to

temple treasurer.

Chauncey experiences his first perceptions

of financial power brokering while controlling the

finances of the temple. Being the buyer of temple

accessories garnered him favors with street vendors,

temple brothers and outside shopkeepers. He

maintained the ledgers and all tithes assessed to

parishioners. The recruitment processes for the

various temples depend on "grass root" level

initiatives. Chauncey analyzed the diagram of the

finances the temples registered on the books and

was impressed with the economic success of the

organization.

The key secret he recognized was the ability of the leaders to mobilize mass groups in pooling funds for community purposes. The acquiring of land and agriculture were key initiatives for many of the economic visions. Groups were often assembled and developed the concept of making their own clothing and footwear. The idea of self-empowerment was a highly promoted theme in the community.

Chauncey was inside the temple office late one night balancing the books and noticed the increase in membership as a result of the financial records. The desk where he sat was covered with books and papers. He sat hunched over a spreadsheet fiddling with a black fountain pen and calculator. He could feel his eye lids get heavy as his head bobbed forward slowly reawakening him to his surroundings. Chauncey decided his learning process would continue tomorrow and decided to head home for the night. He locked up and walked briskly to the bus stop to catch a ride to his place of residence.

As he awaited the bus he could feel a slight chill in the air and he rubbed his arms to generate heat by the motion. The bus soon arrived and he hoped up the steps to an open front seat near the window. As the bus rumbled forward he could hear a group of guys in the back talking. They were in an intense discussion of the plight of black males, and how police brutality was rampant in the neighborhood, due to racial profiling. It was the late 1960's and civil rights issues were the major topic in many communities. He listened intensely as the four men spoke in turns of their resentment of the prevailing system.

Chauncey had heard this type of cipher session before and now that he was in the NOI it seemed strange to hear the talk. He was now enlightened in a way because of his newly acquired knowledge and study of materials not immediately available to the average person. In his opinion this men were dead. They had no knowledge and most likely were not as educated as he was in various issues. He questioned the reasons for what made these men realize the predicament they were in. Was it just the talk among the media and their neighbors? Alternatively, was it that they naturally felt the injustice of the situation?

The bus slowed and stopped near Chauncey's residence. He reached in his pocket and realized he had a temple flyer in his pocket. He decided to give it to one of the guys that were nearest to where he was seated.

"I overheard your conversation and you probably could learn more if you set in on a session down at the temple," said Chauncey.

The man looked down at Chauncey's extended hand with the flyer took it and read it as Chauncey skipped down the steps to exit the bus.

He could feel the guy's eyes on him as the bus pulled off from the stop. He walked towards the old two-story house he considered home.

***

Chauncey thought of the recruitment process and the men he worked with in the neighborhood among the people. They considered the process "teaching and fishing," which was beneficial in seeding the community to support NOI. Most of the new recruits considered this work menial. They were all ambitious and had dreams of becoming a minister of a temple and becoming a force in their own right. Chauncey believed in the concept of not putting the cart before the horse and tried this as essential training.

As he lay in the bed daydreaming he took out a study guide and tried to memorize a passage for lessons the next day. He had taken a shower and his body felt light as he relaxed on the cushioned mattress. He had a study lamp on near his bed which provided a dim reading light for him to see the book pages. He had been told that if a person tries to remember information before falling asleep that they could master memorization of anything. In learning the lesson for the temple it required the reciting of the details of large amounts of data. Chauncey wanted to master this technique and was determined to learn all he could doing this method of data retention.

He nodded and was jolted awake by sound in the hallway. The old military captain was giving one of his renters a good cussing for coming in drunk and throwing up over the entire front porch. The guy was apparently passed out in the hallway and could not be lifted by the old captain.

"Get your drunk ass up and clean this shit up," shouted the old captain in between horrific coughs and dry heaves. Chauncey switched off his reading light and drifted off to sleep.

CHAPTER 4 - Plan in Action

Chauncey spent a couple of years as the treasure of the temple working closely with the minister. He possessed specialized training in administration due to his courses taken on the college level. He was ambitious and desired to be more than just a second string administrator with a boss. He desired a certain type of personal empowerment wanting to own a business which would display his talents. In his works and study in the temple he had analyzed the process of operational functions. The NOI was very successful in sustaining economic self-sufficiency programs. In creating bakeries, restaurants, fish markets, skin care, and lines of hair care products their finances grew without bounds.

Chauncey saw firsthand how beneficial sermons were on controlling the masses of people attending services. The main lectures were done on Sundays and they motivated people for the seven days of the workweek. Mondays were designated for the afternoon meeting of the Fruit of Islam all male paramilitary force. Wednesdays were the mini lecture series with all wannabe ministers giving speeches. Fridays were designed for group study and intellectual exchange between members. Saturdays were the women's trainings classes which often started in the mornings.

Chauncey also participated in the mini lectures held on Wednesday afternoons and had become quite fond of the meetings. He debated other ministers in training and developed his oratorical skills in developing presentations.

* * *

Chauncey decided that once he obtained his degree he would work full time in the temple and perhaps take over finance in the organization as a whole. He had met many national representatives and had cultivated a good working relationship with them. His time in the temple had developed his interpersonal skills at navigating the political strata of the NOI's hierarchy. He soon built credibility with executive level leadership in the temple and among the NOI leadership.

Recognition of temples in the NOI was based upon the temples that profited the most in the organization. The Muhammad Speaks newspaper was the medium that garnered the most street sales. Competition among up and coming ministers were fierce in moving volumes of newspapers on the street. Chauncey in maintaining the temple finances realized that his temple was lagging in that area of

income generation. Being the ambitious person he

was he devised a plan to shift most record revenue

sales to that of the newspaper's in financial

reporting.

Chauncey arrived in the temple early on a

Saturday morning and armed himself with an

armful of Muhammad Speaks newspapers. He

decided he would hit the street corners alone and

sell them all before the afternoon. He bumped into

the temple minister before he got out the door.

"Brother Chauncey I see you got an early

start on things," said the minister.

"Yes sir got to make my sales," Chauncey

replied.

"Listen," said the minister as he cupped his arm over Chauncey shoulder and walked him to the exit.

"The brothers think you're doing an admirable job," he commented. "I want to see you with your own temple soon."

"Thank you sir," said Chauncey as he walked out the door into the morning sunlight.

Chauncey hustled on the streets trying to get people to buy the papers but the process was harder than it looked. The outside heat was debilitating and having a suit and bow tie did not help him in being cool. His feet hurt and his voice was sore from talking to the people he encountered on the street. He returned to the temple at the end of the day with only a portion of the papers sold. He knew he would have to continue to attempt to sell the papers daily but he would make sure to make

adjustments on the financial reports. He was

determined to be recognized as a future top

minister.

NOI annually held national seminars in

which all the temples across the country get

together for a weekend summit. In the summit the

national executive committee meets and

acknowledges the accomplishments of individual

temples. Chauncey reasoned that, if his minister

acknowledged him as the top newspaper salesman,

then maybe he could possibly secure a spot on the

next trip to nationals.

Individuals selling the newspapers could

earn about one hundred or two hundred dollars a

day. As well as acquiring a little notoriety an

individual can earn money to take care of himself

and eat. Among the temples ministers took pride in having their names announced among fellow ministers and parishioners as leaders in FOI business affairs. Ministers vied intensively for the 2nd in command position role in relation to the national minister.

Chauncey's main concern was the vision of ministering from his own temple one day and he would do it by working more than every other prospect minister. The prospects were a very vicious pool of individuals. On the surface they appeared gracious and courteous in the eye of the public. They often do their dirty work behind the backs of their perceived enemies and back stab people when the time arises. Chauncey had a term he often used for these types of people and he called them backbiters.

As Chauncey became recognized as a mover and shaker in the business of temple affairs many haters developed. Grumblers said that he spent too much time in the temple and he was working to unseat the sitting minister. Chauncey paid no mind to these rumors and with his meetings with the temple minister the issue was never raised. Chauncey doubled his efforts at being recognized as the top producer in the temple.

Chauncey was recognized for twelve months of dedicated service in newspaper sales and serving as the temple treasurer. He received honorable mention in the NOI newspaper for his service. There was no physical picture of him but his deeds were noted in the commentary section of the paper. The temple minister spoke boastfully of his accomplishments in service and that only infuriated the competing ministers.

"Because you have distinguished yourself as a natural leader," said the temple minister. "Upon completion of your work here I am putting a recommendation request in for you to be appointed a temple."

This was the news Chauncey had been waiting for and it certainly would garner national recognition in the NOI. The traditional process was that the national minister would make temple appointments during annual conventions and this would certainly allow him to travel with the temple minister to the next convention.

Chauncey knew that they would likely be gunning for him and his position. He widened his circle of associates and became friendly with the new members of the temple. He knew he needed friends and a crew that would have his best interest above that of the other members in the hierarchy.

Chauncey established a late night oratorical group that attracted young members for the purpose of debate contests. The contests usually held every Friday night soon became popular for the new members. It was a place to socialize, and meet people for friendships, to include the opposite sex. This move garnered many supporters for Chauncey and it abated rumors that he was a showboat. Chauncey had effectively erected a hedge around him which backed down the temple backbiters for a while at least.

CHAPTER 5 - Trouble

Chauncey used his college education to excel in finance and business endeavors. He soon began doing freelance consulting with other brothers to earn extra money. He was good at what he did and was paid handsomely for his services. He advised owners of Bakeries, Barber Shops, and Churches on finance bookkeeping. He had honed his skill as a businessman because of his ability to relate to others in slang and speak the talk of business owners. Chauncey was advising a Barber one day of his finances on the East side of Decatur,

"Do you think I can write off my travel expenses when I attend hair care seminars," he inquired.

"Yeah, no problems as long as you keep your receipts," replied Chauncey.

The barber smiled with delight as he heard the news and began shuffling the papers on the table where they were seated. It had been hours and they had poured of the business finances of the shop for a year's term. It was after hours, the shop was empty of patrons, and the sound of a radio played in the background as they worked. The old radio played the melody of an upbeat Rappers Delight song.

"My business is a sole proprietor but I was thinking of making it corporate," stated the Barber.

"I would suggest you go with an S-corp. or an LLC," replied Chauncey. "You're a designated small business and if you have losses in the business claim them personally."

"Besides," said Chauncey. "A C-corporation faced double taxation."

"You college boys know your stuff," said the Barber.

He rose from his chair, grabbed a nearby broom, and began sweeping the floor out of habit. Chauncey noticed that the floor appeared clean and wondered how many times a day the old Barber performed this action. He straightened in his seat and let out a big stretch releasing some tension. The Barber continued to sweep as he hummed the tune playing on the radio.

"You know you should really try to get your own thing going," said the Barber as he continued to sweep not looking up from his work.

"A man with your skills would be a good leader to folks in this community," he said.

Chauncey knew the man was right in his assessment and he had considered the option many times prior. He could do private lectures for individuals separate from the temple meetings and establish his own flock of parishioners. He was making good money doing consulting and could more than double his earning potential holding small lectures on his acquired knowledge in the NOI.

Chauncey exited the barbershop and he immediately spotted a dark colored sedan across the street with its engine running. It was dark outside and the streets were disserted with no one in sight. He would not have noticed the car otherwise but because it was running his interested was peaked. He could not see inside the car because the windows were limo tint and no light could penetrate inside. He continued walking towards the bus stop and assumed it was the temple brothers keeping tabs on him. He could hear the engine of the car reeve up as it was put into gear and it pulled down a side alley street into obscurity.

Chauncey knew he would have to cover his financial tracks as well as his social ones. He could feel the eyes of the brothers watching him and the rumors were already swirling about his movements. He caught the MARTA back to his pad and was conscious of all the people he encountered getting home. As he entered his residence he took his mail from the mailbox and noticed a letter from the temple. He pushed open his room door and plopped down on the bed to open the letter. It was on official temple letterhead and the first line read, "You are suspended pending investigation of allegations of embezzlement." He could not read the rest of the letter because of shock and disgust.

***

It was a Saturday afternoon and Chauncey entered the temple to confront the minister concerning the letter he received the prior day. The women were having their usual weekend meeting and he proceeded to the back office. The minister was seated at his desk when he barged through the door and dropped the letter on his desk.

"After all my efforts and I got told of my suspension by a letter in the mail," said Chauncey.

The minister adjusted his glasses and reared back in his office chair. He looked at the crumpled letter on his desk and removed his glasses. He took a handkerchief from his pocket and began cleaning one lens.

"The brothers are saying you may have come into some money," he said with his head down continuing to clean the lens of his spectacles.

"What business is that of the brothers," exclaimed Chauncey. "I work, consult, and help businessmen in this community."

"We're just suspending you from your position as treasurer while we have a look at the books, that's all," replied the minister placing his glasses back on and looking Chauncey squarely in the face.

"No disrespect sir," he said to the minister. "You can tell the brothers to keep their hands out of my pocket."

He turned and walked out of the office seething with anger. He walked past the temple women and knew it was the last time he would see

them in their white tunics. He walked out of the
temple knowing he was walking away from that life
for good.

***

Chauncey began holding his own lectures in
the basement of neighborhood public library. He
espoused the tenants of what he learned in the NOI
and mingled it with financial self-reliance
teachings. A few of his supporters from the temple
attended his sessions and he did not hear much of
the so-called investigations of his alleged financial
misdealing in regards to the temple. One night after
he completed a lecture he was accosted by three
brothers from the temple on his way home.

"You stole teachings from the minister,"
said one man as he attempted to shove Chauncey.

Chauncey kept himself in shape and had
done many jujitsu trainings with the FOI. He
instantly spun around and caught the man in the
neck with the bottom side of his foot. He wore a
pair of hard-bottomed Stacy Adams and the man
went down like a sack of potatoes. The second
brother attempted to grab him and he chopped him
in the throat causing the man to cough up blood in a
profuse manner. Chauncey felt as if he was moving
in slow motion and knew he was out numbered
three to one. If he could not equalize the fight by
using his speed it would be a lost cause for him.
The third man stood with his back toward a brick
wall and Chauncey wondered why he was not
charging him. Chauncey jumped straight up in the
air and kicked the brother snapping his head back
into the wall. The man head bounced off the wall

and he lay motionless on the sidewalk. Chauncey looked over the stretched out bodies of the men and hit a quick stride home.

"Did you see that, he moved like a cat on those brothers," he heard a person said as he rounded the street corner home.

Chauncey did not consider himself a violent person but he was well adept at protecting himself. While many he hung around felt controversy was a way of life he himself yearned for peace. He rationed people instinctively desired well being and if he could embody this concept in his teachings it would be more attractive. He also rationed the concept of the peaceful warrior theory. This leader would possess exceptional combat skills but prefer peaceful resolutions to conflict.

Chauncey knew he would have those haters who would not be happy with him branching doing his own thing. He did not believe he would encounter retaliation against his young movement. He felt regret in perpetrating violence against the ones that looked like him and he repented in his heart.

He heard footsteps behind him as he walked and turned for more confrontation. He saw a young man who recoiled upon seeing his facial expression.

"Hey man, no trouble. Can you teach me those moves," the man inquired.

"I simply defended myself," Chauncey replied.

Chauncey knew that the young man would not be content with this response and searched his pocket for an extra flyer for his basement lectures.

He pulled one from his pocket and gave it to the man.

"I lecture and you can learn more about me by reading this," said Chauncey.

The man took the flyer and looked it over.

"Thanks," he replied.

CHAPTER 6 - Restart

Chauncey knew he had to get out of town and was unsure what to do about his predicament. The brothers in the temple were watching his every move and he felt as if his life was in danger. He considered relocation and he was interested in a place that was conducive to his personal ambitions. As he sat pondering his situation in his small apartment he could hear the ramblings of people wandering the halls. He heard a man yell out and he could hear the old captain curse the air. Someone had a small radio and it was playing snippets of a news broadcast.

"Riots have broken out in Miami Florida," said the news broadcaster. "Police murdered a black insurance salesman and the Negroes burned

down Liberty City."

Many cities across America were

experiencing cultural clashes among ethnicities and

civil unrest was not a surprise. Chauncey listened

to the report and realized that his services could be

used to mobilize the community of that city.

Mobilization also meant money and an opportunity

to build his own organization.

Atlanta represented the royalty of civil rights

movement in comparison to other American cities.

Chauncey experienced first-hand how black

mobilized on Auburn Avenue to develop effective

black leadership. Student leadership was an

emerging power in the city and Chauncey aligned

himself with that movement for realization of a

dream. Sweet Auburn had a heavy influence on

how Chauncey desired to build his organization and he would utilize all his skills to reach his goal.

Chauncey arose from his chair, looked around his dwelling for his luggage case, and began packing a few of his things. He decided he would leave for Miami in the next couple of days. He would secure his bus ticket and slip out under the cover of darkness as to avoid the all-seeing eyes of the brothers.

It was the mid-seventies and defectors from communist Cuba were flooding Miami neighborhoods and acquiring vocational training for work in the community. Many professionals and entrepreneurs from Cuba established successful endeavors with the use of federal funds to defray the cost of transportation and resettlement. The federal programs such as minority business set-asides established for blacks as a result of civil

rights were awarded to the newly arrived refugees.

Blacks complained bitterly and deemed it as

poaching by the white newcomers on their

entitlements. As the Hispanics displaced blacks

from jobs and formed businesses for their people

brutality by the police increased in Liberty City.

This comprised the social setting when

Chauncey touched down in Miami to organize

blacks in the community. With Cuban refugees

becoming naturalized they voted winning majorities

pushing blacks out of the city's mayor-ship, public

school superintendent, and county district attorney,

city council positions.

Chauncey's plan was simple and he

reformed his beliefs to mesh the old books of the

bible with Islamic teachings. He would start with

one perspective member and reach followers one at
a time. Chauncey took to the street corners of 62nd
Avenue and 7th preaching the word to all passers-
by. He was on the corner one sunny day and
spotted a woman sitting at the bus stop fanning herself because of the intense heat. He approached her
and smiled widely at the woman.

"Do you believe in god," he asked.

The woman stopped fanning herself with her
hand and looked at him with a blank expression.

"Yes, I do," was her reply.

"Then I would like you to join my
movement to convince others of our belief," he said
to the woman.

He scooted next to the woman on the bus
bench and began his mini-lecture on the importance
of belief and self-empowerment for blacks.

Unbeknownst to him there stood a man on the side of the stop listening to their conversation.

Chauncey stipulated no use of dope and alcohol as tenements of his philosophy and the listeners were impressed. Heroin and pot use were well known in the community long before the crack epidemic arrived in Liberty City.

The woman on the bench whom Chauncey had engaged in discussion was Elizabeth Cordell. She worked as a secretary and lived with her three kids in an efficiency apartment in Liberty City. She was a hard working woman and she, like other Miamians, were disillusioned with the way her community was treated by government officials. Chauncey was successful in winning her over and they became partners. He saw an immediate advantage in being affiliated with Elizabeth. He would seek to utilize her ability as a secretary and

her knowledge of the local community. The

gentleman that eaves dropped on the two at the bus

stop was Lester Poole. He soon became a convert

to Chauncey's way of thinking and spread the word

among people he knew.

Chauncey walked the sidewalks of the

blighted neighborhoods of Liberty City and in his

strolls he attracted spectators. He soon dropped the

bow tie and clean cut image of the NOI and resorted

to wearing white robes and a white head wrap. He

began to dress like the people from the bible.

People would see him in the streets and marvel at

the way he was dressed during his lengthy sermons.

He sometimes carried a bullhorn and would shout

out scriptures as he toured the hood. People

assumed he was crazy initially but his words would

hang in their thoughts holding his message of empowerment.

Chauncey teamed up with another street preacher known as Brother Love and held weekly services from an old abandoned warehouse in the hood. He and Brother Love developed a racket during their long services by selling beef patties and soliciting offerings to help their cause. They made good money and soon acquired a rental lease for daily gatherings of their parishioners.

One afternoon two men entered the storefront building Brother Love and Chauncey were renting for their service. The aisles of the chairs were arranged in a circle as they entered and they could hear drumming coming from the back of the room. The walls were lined with pictures of biblical saints and they were all of black ancestry.

"Anyone here," one of the men yelled out.

Brother Love walked from around a wall in the rear of the room. The drumming had stopped and he possessed a small drum under his left arm. The two men looked at each other and with a wry smile one of them spoke.

"Is pastor Chauncey around," the man asked in a sarcastic tone.

"No, who are you?" replied Brother Love.

"Friends of the brother," the man said.

The man who had not spoken slipped behind Brother Love. Brother Love looked perplexed and noticed the men seemed out of place and assumed they were from out of town.

"I'm brother Love, maybe I can send a message for you," he said.

"You sure can," the man replied.

The man behind Brother Love snatched the wooden drum from under his arm and smashed it squarely upon his head. Brother Love dropped like a sack of potatoes and cried out for help. The man bludgeoned the old spiritual leader to death and as he lay sprawled out blood crept over the floor of the room like a thick layer of house paint. The man dropped the crumpled drum on the floor beside the body. He bent over, dipped his finger in a pool of it, and wrote on a nearby wall. They then exited the storefront in silence, unseen, out the rear entrance of the building.

Hours later Chauncey showed up to the storefront to see it surrounded by police and paramedics. He entered the building and was immediately questioned by uniformed police and detectives.

"Do you know this man," a cop inquired.

"Yeah, he's my friend," replied Chauncey.

"He was your friend," the cop replied. "You know what happened here?"

"No, I just got here," said Chauncey.

"Look over here at this," said a detective.

He pointed at a near-by wall, and written on the wall were words: *Get your hands out of my pockets nigga,* Chauncey felt a hot knot of something rise up in his throat, and he wanted to vomit.

"You know who did this," asked the detective.

"No," said Chauncey.

Chauncey knew instantly what this was about upon gazing at the message scrawled in blood on the walls of the storefront. He felt guilt that

Brother Love experienced such a violent end. He

knew the brothers from ATL were violent but he

didn't think it would lead to the death of an

innocent person. He resolved not to tell the police

anything and offered no leads to the investigators.

He would let them do the job they were paid to do

by the community and pray for the soul of Brother

Love.

Chauncey, determined he needed protection,

formulated a plan to have an inner circle he named

the magnificent seven. He recruited ex-football

players, convicts, and bodyguards as a part of the

group. He offered them specialized teachings and

other perks to motivate the bunch. They carried

five-foot oak wood staffs and some had machetes

that could cut through wood. Although the death of

Brother Love deeply affected the flock they rallied

closer to Chauncey and dedicated tributes such as tithes among other monies. He felt he needed a fortification for his movement and plans were formulated.

Chauncey's group grew in numbers and he sought to cultivate more stringent relationships with the group. He purchased an old abandoned warehouse and converted it into living quarters for faithful parishioners. He made it a requirement for the new tenants to give up worldly possessions to the group. People sold their homes, land, and emptied bank accounts pooling it for the benefit of the group. Chauncey's wealth grew and his followers became known around the city as the Sufis or the wooly haired ones. They all donned long white garments and white head wrap turbines. They bought and owned grocery stores, laundry

mats, car washes, and restaurants in the hood.
Many of their buildings were painted white and they
operated as a well-organized group in the
community.

Chauncey ran the organization in an
efficient manner, and with the help of Elizabeth as
his partner, business was good. He believed in
professionalism and was of the opinion that this
mode of operation parodies the big businesses of
America. Having a checks and balance system of
administration was a great benefit which allowed
for the elimination of wasteful processes. This in
essence is the setup of the government and all its
departments. The years rolled by and as the Sufi
organizations prospered with wealth and power
Chauncey took on a new name. He adopted the
name Sufi El Cid or Wooly Head Chief.

CHAPTER 7 - Momentum

Sufi El Cid's followers built his organization by going door-to-door in the black communities of Overton, Liberty City, and Little Haiti. The word of mouth style of recruitment seemed very effective. Many of those recruited came from a broken background and from among the city's poor residents. However, collectively they were a force to be reckoned with proving there is force in numbers.

"Shalom," said Sufi El Cid as he greeted new parishioners entering the compound.

He stood near the front entrance and the magnificent seven were at his side. Their white robes flapped as a breeze swept through the opened front gate. There was a mural painted at the entrance of a futuristic city populated by black folk, complete with flying saucers. Painted below it was the phrase, "The black Christ is risen among us today to deliver us from the illuminate." The compound was located in the heart of Liberty City and it spanned an entire city block. The group had renovated the warehouse into partitioned off condo settlements. They'd established food stores, clothing shops, a school, health clinic, and a temple. A print shop in the compound employed many of the parishioners that gave up their jobs. The print shop earned the Sufi nation money as well as the many bakeries, grocery stories and laundry places.

Later that night El Cid was scheduled to address the new residents of the compound with a great welcome speech. All the residents were assembled in the banquet hall located in the center of the compound. He was escorted by the seven and led on stage among the many observers.

"Tonight we welcome all new residents of the compound," said El Cid as his voice boomed through the speakers assembled in the various corners of the compound.

The crowd consisted of children, teenagers, young adults, old grandmothers and fathers who had given all to move into the make shift city. They were average everyday people looking for some special meaning to their lives. They thought they had identified that realization in joining the Sufi nation.

The new residents beamed with delight while the crowd gathered around to congratulate them. They were unsure of what they were getting into but like the rest they sought purpose. They were breaking from the normalcy of everyday nine to five living and defining a new reality for themselves.

"First thing is first," stated El Cid, "Now the Rules."

"All men will practice abstinence while living on compound ground," he stated.

"Women will succumb to mid wife education practices, the youth must attend school, all able body men are required to work, and temple service is mandatory," he said.

There was a murmur that went through the crowd and people looked from one to the other. The new recruits looked a bit nervous but no one voiced an opinion. The magnificent seven gripped their staffs and looked about for any objections. The crowded settled and was silent.

El Cid's partner Elizabeth was second in command and she monitored all business transactions of the organization. The new comers had pledged all personal income toward them establishing residency in the compound. The men worked in the print shop. The women became teachers in the schools and help run the compound businesses. El Cid's residence in the compound was an elaborate tent with red carpet leading up to the entrance. Well guarded by two members of the seven it contained all the modern conveniences of a normal house.

El Cid led the mid wife education forums and would sometimes select women for advanced private tutorials. He led discussions on the proper way to douche and demonstrated it on volunteers. He also read from medical books the proper way of delivering babies. He selected one of the newcomers for a private lesson and they entered the bedroom area of his tent.

The young woman was tall and voluptuous. She was barely out of her teens with beautiful brown eyes. Her thighs were well muscled and was slightly visible under the free flowing dress she wore. El Cid had noticed her during his welcome speech to the group and could barely keep his eyes off her.

"I'm glad you joined us," said El Cid, "Relax and have a seat."

The young woman sat on the bed and El Cid poured her a cup of herbal tea he had brewing just for this moment.

"What's your name?" He asked.

"Laura," she replied.

"Are you married?" he asked.

"Yes," she said.

"Well that's good. We need to build this movement with young strong children and by having natural child births it can be done." He commented.

He took the teacup she sipped from and placed it on a nearby table. As she sat on the bed he knelt in front of her and slipped his hands up under her dress. Her well-formed thighs gave him an instant hard on. He gently spread her legs while talking to her as he worked up under her dress.

"With the right techniques of posture you can experience almost no pain during natural child birth," he said.

He slid his hands up the young woman's thighs over her buttocks to the rim of her panties and attempted to slide them off. The woman had largely been unresponsive to El Cid the entire time. At this moment he would test her to see if she wanted it by tempting her with the possibility of sex with him. As he slipped his fingers inside the bands of her panties she raised her bottom and he slipped her panties off. El Cid smiled to himself and would now handle business.

El Cid sat in his tent reading scriptures preparing for the evening sermon when Elizabeth entered.

"Chauncey, we need to talk," she said.

He looked up from his work and with his eyes he silently scolded her. He paused before saying anything.

"I've told you a thousand times about calling me by a government name," he said.

"Well Sufi El Cid, we need to talk," she corrected herself.

"What," he remarked.

"The men of the camp are not happy with the abstinence rule and I think this could cause real problems," she said.

"They're under my roof and they follow my rules," he replied.

"Some of them are married and besides the rumor is you're the one who's not abiding by the abstinence edict," she commented.

"This is not about me. It's about building a meaningful movement and to do that there has to be discipline among the file and rank. If I can instill discipline using the most desired of their passions I have made an indestructible force." He said.

"What about the women?" She asked.

"I said nothing about the women," he commented not looking up from his work.

All parishioners were encouraged to cut off any relationship that went against the teachings of the Sufi movement. Some individuals went as far as cutting communications with their loved ones. Complete surrender and commitment to the cause was instilled in each, and every, member. El Cid required all members to be productive in the movement by engaging in meaningful work. Members not employed inside the compound staffed the grocery stores and shops around the city owned by the Sufis. The people staffed in the compound print shop made flyers that were distributed promoting the aims of the movement. Publications were also sold for money to be place in

Sufi coffers to sustain compound functions and livelihoods.

During the daylight hours members were active at their jobs and inside the compound children were instructed in Sufism. Everyone was busy and El Cid made sure that all kept to his or her assigned schedule. When the workday was over the afternoon consisted of kosher dinners, clean up time, and nightly study sessions. El Cid led the study groups that reinforced his laws and taught on the history of black folks.

El Cid had much free time to study the religions of Buddhism, Judaism, Sikhism, Hinduism, and others in formulating his theology. He had used the freewill of others to forge a movement dedicated to empowering the disenfranchised of Miami. He talked a lot about concentrated group thought and the laws of

attractions. He would quote many scriptures from

Leviticus.

"If you reject my decrees and abhor my laws

and fail to carry out all my commands and so

violate my covenant, then I will do this to you: I

will bring upon you sudden terror, wasting diseases

and fever that will destroy your sight and drain

away your life," he said in a nightly study group.

El Cid built the movement into a multi-

million dollar organization and was in consultation

with his elders to establish satellite chapters in other

cities. It was now the 1990s and mega churches

were based in most large metropolitan cities. El Cid

was confident that his message could reach

disenfranchised blacks in these locations. He

believed his theology would begin a revival in this

enlightenment age. He would train his elders and send emissaries to carry his word.

El Cid controlled the lives of those who followed him totally and from 5am to dusk they toiled for the efforts of the Sufi nation under his watchful eye. The Sufi nation had acquired land, rental properties, and other business. Many in the community were aware of the growing number of converts to the movement. Some were unaware of the submission required by El Cid. For many the wealth of the movement was enough to entice them to join. El Cid was successful in creating a singular reality for members. Any one that deviated from the plan was dealt with in a swift and efficient manner. The Magnificent Seven were the storm troopers dispensed at the will of El Cid to deal with any situations.

The word cult was being attached to any movement outside of the major religions and outsiders considered El Cid's followers as this. Many government figures were uneasy with the success of the organization. They did respect the numbers the movement wielded in the community. It was apparent that people were discontent and yearned for something more in their lives. El Cid was successful in organizing these masses and coordinating programs to make them functional. Leaders recognized El Cid as a successful leader and desired to befriend him for their own purposes. His group could help sway public opinion and that power alone attracts attention.

CHAPTER 8 - Soldiers

The Magnificent Seven maintained order and carried out the wishes of El Cid. Many in the organization were hesitant to speak out because of them. They were intimidating with their 6 foot staffs and all of them were muscle bound women and men over 6 feet tall. They enforced camp curfews and imposed penalties on those in opposition of Sufi law. They trained in the martial arts while weight-training workouts kept them in top physical condition.

"In violation of Sufi law I sentence you to seven lashes," said El Cid to an elderly man in his early sixties.

The man was discovered having sex with a female whom he was not committed too in marriage. Sufi law demanded celibacy except for in certain circumstances of marriage and procreation. The women were exempt from the law and only men were held to this standard. The men of the Magnificent Seven prostrated the man over a chair. While he was bent over the chair the women of the seven took a wide oak paddle with holes in it and paddled him.

Whack! The sound of the man's bare ass being hit with the wood echoed through the room. One of the stockier women of the seven took her time with administering her lick during a turn. She spread her well-muscled legs like a baseball player's stance and raised the paddle like a bat. As she swung the air whistled through the holes of the paddle and came down hard on the man's behind.

* * *

Whack! The man let out a low groan and tried to maintain his manhood by not letting a tear go.

Another woman of the seven doused the man's rear end with water and then took her swing. Whack! The sound vibrated the windowpanes and the paddle skid the top of the man's bare rear sliding from her hand. It hit the back of the wall as observers scattered to get out of the way.

The women of the Magnificent Seven were just as brutal as their male counterparts and El Cid demanded it. Punishment was one of the ways he maintained power and kept his flock in line. He singled out disrupters and called them Uncle Tom's and Sambos. No one dared to go against him publicly. However, dissenters were active in the compound and his network of spies informed El Cid of their movements.

***

Duff was once a Sunday school teacher in the compound and because he could not adapt to the celibacy laws of the camp he was kicked out. Many of the dissenters of the group met at his residence and talked of the goings on with the movement. He maintained friends in the camp and often went back for visits. Many of the dissenters thought that El Cid was going too far with the ideology of his movement and believed himself as god on earth. They spoke of the total control he had over their lives. They spoke of how El Cid had demanded the fingers and ears of blasphemers chopped off. They said El Cid required body parts to be delivered as proof of an individual's commitment to the movement.

Duff himself experienced the overbearing rule of El Cid and could sympathize with the dissenters. In providing his place as a regular meeting spot the numbers of those that were not happy with their condition doubled. Word got back to El Cid about Duff and the influence he was gaining in the camp although he was kicked out of the movement.

The Magnificent Seven were alerted that if they spotted Duff they were to put him down. The members warned Duff that El Cid was not happy about his affiliations with the dissenters. His friends advised him to avoid the compound until things died down but El Cid's spies proved to be quite resourceful. He was spotted visiting a female friend of his in the compound and immediately the Seven were dispatched.

"It's Friday the 13th Duff, what're you doing here," said one of the member of the Seven.

Duff had just walked out of a bungalow and was heading toward the gate when confronted by the Seven. He looked around the immediate area for a weapon, a bottle, or stick but the area was clean.

"I'm leaving and I want no problems with you all," he said.

Two men grabbed him from behind and jerked him up behind a nearby dumpster in the back of the compound. Duff kicked and tried to wrestle free from the men's grip but could not. They had him tight and his heart sank at the thought of the beating he would have to endure at their hands.

"We finally got you boy and we're going to teach you a lesson," said one of the men.

One man put Duff in a headlock and two others began kicking him furiously in the side of his ribs. Duff continued to struggle and the men kicked harder trying to subdue all efforts of his struggle. Duff began coughing up blood and could feel the strain on his neck as the man tightened the grip around his head.

"Hold still boy," said the third man.

He continued to kick and Duff struggled eventually freeing himself from the man that had him in the headlock. He was struck in the face, with the staff of life, and fell to the floor, face down. The staff of life was made of oak and was carried by the Seven for infliction of the deadliest of pain on victims.

"Turn him over," said one of the men.

The cement ground was covered in bright red blood and Duff lay in a heap. He was breathing hard and was tired from the exhaustion of the ordeal. The two men drug his limp body out of the compound.

"Get this cleaned up and use red paint if it doesn't come up," They said to the third man.

Duff was thrown on the back of a pickup truck and driven to a disserted field in the glades.

"Please don't kill me," he said to the men.

"You know the creed," said one man.

The man shoved his head down and drew a moon shaped sword from the inside of his belt. With one swift motion he attempted to chop off Duff's head but the blade got caught in the wind pipe and an airy gurgling noise could be heard.

"Damn this blade is dull," said the man.

"Use mine," said the second man handing over his sword.

Chop! The head rolled off the old tree stump and the men stood back from the body as it twitched on the ground.

"We gotta take the head back," said the man holding the bloody sword.

"I got a plastic bag," said the other man as he scooped the head into the bag.

El Cid demanded trophies of those dispatched in his name. Duff's head would represent the pinnacle of his power. It would also mark the resoluteness of his dissenters in seeing him removed from power. As news of the violent death of Duff spread among the followers many were preparing to go to the authorities.

Many believed the line had been crossed by

the El Cid regime and were hesitate about

congregating to outright protest the matter. Some

would be successful in contacting the outside for

help and El Cid would exercise all measures to

expose those few. Absolute power corrupts

absolutely and the followers of El Cid had a front

row seat in experiencing this phenomenon.

CHAPTER 9 - The Dream

El Cid sat in his study reading an old King James Version of the Bible and jotted down notes as he went through the pages. He was alone and the room was quiet except for a clock tic- tocking in the background. His elaborate tent was well lit with burning oil lamps and incense. He sat at an ornately designed desk with sculptures of angels fighting dragons in artwork patterns. His study was walled with books and papyruses which he collected from his travels around the world. He desired to construct an initiation for his followers through his teachings. He didn't want it to be just another instruction or lesson. He wanted to increase his following and captivate minds.

In studying various biographies of great leaders and teachers, he discovered the difference between instruction and initiation. Instruction was nothing more than a teaching of processes and fact stating. Learning by initiation creates an experience that's personal to the student. The message has to make sense to the person learning and by figuring out the lesson it's more valuable to the learner. Only when holding back, then simply telling someone what they want to know, will the method be maximized. He thought back to his time in Atlanta, studying under the NOI, and how relevant that experience was to him.

As he prepared his scripture teachings for his flock he thought of the concept of accessibility. In making himself accessible to his followers he could build deep personal bonds with people.

• • •

Making oneself scarce adds perceived value but it creates a distance with the masses. El Cid wanted total control so his approach was based on the personal appeal of relating to folks. His teachings would combine old scripture with modern concepts and nomenclature for an increased affect.

El Cid knew the importance of remaining calm in the face of uncertainty and used this technique in his lectures. When unforeseen outburst occurred he controlled the occurrence with the assistance of well-placed anecdotal phrases and secret knowledge quotes. In doing this he was perceived by many as always in control of things.

Many of El Cid's followers also spoke of his detach nature which gave impressions that it was more to him than just his mere physical presence. Many people told him this and he used it to heighten his profile as a spiritual leader. His dream

was that of a leader of men and he wanted to

accomplish this at all costs.

He thought back to his old colleague Brother

Love and his concept teaching of "Chunk Up."

Whenever they were among the congregation he

would always think in bigger terms than the

parishioners would. Once a parishioner asked,

"How was your day?" He replied, "I woke up this

morning, I'm blessed." When someone talked of

taking up collections for the temple building fund,

he spoke of purchasing a new site. His was often

perceived as focusing on the bigger picture of

things. El Cid had learned this valuable lesson from

him and it was paying off in a big way.

El Cid made sure his lessons alluded to the

mysterious texts of religious philosophy and the

books of the bible. As he learned more about the knowledge of ancient texts he acquired a god-like confidence which empowered him to demand the unthinkable of people. He successfully appealed to their needs and wants in all of his ramblings. His lectures were constructed to reflect his intellect, genius, and creativity. These tools would allow for the development of an effective cult thought El Cid in his musings. His thoughts were like machine gun ammo as he rifled them onto paper at the ornate desk. He originally planned to jot down one-line phrases but it developed into long sheets. He knew that this lecture would be a memorable one and would weed out any non-believers. He was motivated to cultivate true believers in fulfillment of his dream.

The parishioners of the movement were desperate for hope and believed that El Cid could deliver on his promises of salvation. They were a cast of ordinary people with jobs and mortgages in the mundane world of 9 to 5 living. They were bored and wished for fortune in their lives. They searched for meaning in their existence in America and found it in the teachings of El Cid. Many were from the drug-infested ghettos and societies downtrodden. In the movement they were somebody and had meaning.

El Cid's teachings changed and grew as his congregation increased. His words were well researched and orchestrated in a way that touched his followers. He said what was on the minds of his followers. His distracters also increase with the growth of the congregation and many admired his

teachings. However, his practices became
questionable in everyday living in the compound.

Local politicians were compelled to
acknowledge El Cid because of his growing
influence among the poorer masses of the
community. Along with their recognition came a
new lot of upper class inquisitors. The numbers of
the movement were very attractive to vote seekers
in Miami's political arena. El Cid realized he could
be a major power broker in leveraging his
movement for political gains. While the individuals
in the movement were powerless to the system they
were still relevant. As a mobilized group they could
effect change and progression in their own
communities. In combining their finances and
considering group needs they built their own
economy. The key was a self-sustaining economy

base which would attract possible investors for continued growth. Many of the local politicians give and expect returns on what is given.

El Cid realized his growing power and became increasingly suspicious of those around him. He had not really planned for the level of growth that was occurring in his organization and knew that he had to determine who could really be trusted in his circle. In many great organizations exist opposition and sublevel division. The current dissidents in the organization were attempting to undermine the dream and El Cid was desperate to stop it.

El Cid excommunicated all individuals he suspected of subversive activities in the compound. The Magnificent Seven were viewed as a group of mindless zombies that half the time operated of their own accord. El Cid ultimately used this group as a control device and seldom gave direct instructions on their enforcement activities.

He pondered the significance of having such a storm troop and likened them to the Israelite army of Moses. He concluded all organizations needed some type of security mechanism to insure order. Order was the thing that caused effective working in a process and he would instill order to the Sufi nation.

Elizabeth was his closest advisor in the movement and while she was competent he was uncertain of her loyalty. She maintained the financial functions and coordinated all fiscal policies. El Cid was careful not to give her total control and ultimately he still approved ultimate decisions concerning fiscal matters.

El Cid rose from his desk and walked to the entrance of his elaborate abode. He could see the Seven entering the compound and advancing in his direction. The guards at his tent were on heightened alert as to the dissident threat. The group of men continued their approach and one possessed a wooden box under his arm. The men were speaking in hush tone and seemed animated in their demeanor.

El Cid stepped back from the doorway and returned to his desk. He finished the last line in the paragraph he constructed and closed the book. He sat with his fingers clasped together in the geometric shape of the pyramid as the men descended on his location.

* * *

CHAPTER 10 - The Rough Patch

Rob Ross was a down and out ex-NBA basketball player who fell under the spell of the Sufi movement. His 6 foot four inch muscular frame made him standout among the members and he was quickly inducted into the Magnificent Seven. He had a sketchy background of petty theft and larceny after his days in the big league. He had come to the movement after serving a short prison stint for check forgery. Rob had led the violent attack against Duff, and now headed to El Cid's domicile holding a wooden box.

Rob had arrived to the compound from the west coast and had come from a broken home as a child. His father was an abusive drunk and after stints of beating his mother left the family when he was two years old. This was one of the major demons that haunted Rob Ross his entire life leading him to his current condition.

Rob devoted his entire existence to the movement and he had nothing else going for him. He lived in the compound and worked at the print shop under the elders of El Cid's inner circle. He worked hard to garner their attention. His superiors soon recognized that he was as a producer and acknowledged his prowess. In volunteering his services and extra time to outside duties of the movement many liked him. He soon was recruited as a member of the Magnificent Seven and his ambition was lit.

Rob had heard the rumors that to earn the call as a true follower of El Cid one must become a death angel. Death angels were members that committed murder as proof of their devotion to El Cid and they kept body parts as evidence of their deed. They often focused on the dregs of society such as the homeless, drug dealers, or junkies. These types of individuals received little attention from media and law enforcement. The death angels helped to solidify control in the compound as well and El Cid's power expanded through this fear.

Rob was inspired to commit the most ruthless acts to be acknowledged as the top follower and he wanted El Cid to know his level of commitment to the cause. There were many ruthless thugs in the Seven and he worked hard to rise to the top of them all.

***

"Are you really going to try to carry that

head with you," inquired one of the Seven to Rob.

"You bet," he quickly shot back.

"I'm going to prove myself to El Cid and

this is going to do it," he stated.

He had wrapped the head in newspaper after

the killing and transported to their current

rendezvous site outside of Alligator Alley. The

news paper was getting soggy from the blood and

was becoming unbearable to transport. The other

members looked on in disgust as Rob fumbled the

head around outside of the opened door of the truck.

"I need a wood box," commented Rob.

It was pitch dark on the roadway and the

only lights came from the vehicle as the group

stopped just off the highway. Rob placed the soggy

newspaper in a section of tall grass unwrapping it because it leaked in the interior of the truck. He took piece by piece of the paper off and the head was now in full display. Blood seeped from the base of a portion of neck and a few vein dangled under the cranium. Some of the members were infuriated that he had taken it and rebuked him for removing it from the body.

Rob looked around the ground and saw some plywood in a heap just off to the side of the road. He gathered up all he could and began to fashion a small box to carry the head. He went back to the truck and fetched some tools. The members smoked cigarettes and shot him cold looks while waiting for him to finish. Rob didn't let the attitude of the group get to him. He was focused and that was what had gotten him this far. He assembled the box and placed the head into it. He carefully

discarded the newspaper deep in the woods off the

side of the road and returned to the truck with box

in hand.

"You should have painted that box," said

one of the members.

There was a chuckle from the group

throughout the truck but Rob was not one of the

ones laughing. As they rode along he was in his

own thoughts. It did not really register that they

had taken the life of another. He felt as if he was

sleepwalking and a part of the lengthy dream

clouded with the feelings of self-doubt. The truck

fell silent as they rumbled on in the darkness.

***

All members contributed to the greater good

of the movement and El Cid utilized his educational

background to build the organization. Street peddlers worked 18-hours a day making sales with Sufi trinkets and if they didn't make the quota they were banished to the prayer room for hours of remedial prayer. They were watched over by the Seven and if they got off their knees before the lauded time they were whipped. El Cid often switched the feeding schedule of the compound to one serving a day. It would often consist of a cup of beans. Many were outraged when their children became emaciated from hunger but no one posed a challenge outright. He would use the extra money for business endeavors. El Cid used all revenues reinvesting it into ventures such as motels, apartment complexes, and real estate.

El Cid garnered a lot of respect in the community, becoming known as king of the ghetto, among community residents. His organization was reported to be worth about 8.5 million and represented Miami's largest black-owned corporation. The mayor of Miami even honored him with an honorary day of the week, "El Cid Day." Many community leaders sought him out when they desired to get photo ops in the community. Where ever a Sufi business was located in the community the drug problem was nonexistent.

The front of an upstanding community activists/responsible businessman was what the public saw of the movement. The surrounding community and residents knew the real story of the movement and its members. Brainwashed members walked around the inner city in their white robes. Their hemmed bottoms swept the ground as they sold trinkets to non-suspecting pedestrians. El Cid

was now an unseen force in the ghetto of Miami.

He put in the footwork of recruiting people to his

way of life and had graduated to a point where his

organization ran itself. Many personally believed

this affected the way he began to view society.

Controlling other people's lives and having the

power to dictate events in favor of certain outcomes

was intoxicating. El Cid often times referred to

himself as god and went as far as describing himself

as god on earth. The people of the community were

very aware as to avoid any run-ins with the group.

The Sufi nation began to grow and reach beyond the

boarder of its Miami genesis.

    Rob Ross as the chief enforcer for the

Magnificent Seven had the ear of El Cid and

directed all movement that called for brute force. El

Cid had acquired the mortgage to quaint house located in Opa-locka and was having trouble with the tenants. Rob took a few of the Seven and was going to do El Cid a favor by evicting the dwellers. He pulled into the driveway of the home and approached the door of the house with another cult member. The neighborhood was quiet and no cars were in the yard or in sight as they waited after knocking on the door. Rob could see the curtain in the window of the house pull back slightly as someone looked out. Just as they thought no one was home the door opened and a middle-aged black man stepped out holding a bat behind his back.

"You Sufi get the hell out my yard," he yelled.

Rob played no games by the time of his development into the chief enforcer of the

Magnificent Seven. He was truly deranged and
having power did not cure his deviant thought
process which was often flawed. He looked the
man in the eye took a step back and drew his 38
revolver pistol.

"Shoot me mother fucker," said the man. "I
ain't scared."

Pop, pop, pop echoed through the quiet
neighborhood as Rob and his partners scrambled
into the vehicle and tore away from the house.
They didn't wait around to see the body hit the
ground but unbeknownst to them the man's wife
was home and saw the men running to the truck.
She quickly called the authorities and they were
arrested near the compound in Liberty City.

Rob sat in a small white room with padded
walls. The A/C was on full blast and he shivered a

bit from the cold air. Two cops walked in and one dropped a thick manila folder on a nearby table. It hit with a thud as the other cop sat facing him.

"We got you boy," said the rosy faced cop.

"A witness placed you at the scene as the trigger man," said the cop who slammed the folder on the table.

"With your record you're up the creek," he said.

"You gonna rat," the other cop inquired.

The cop stood over Rob and glared down at him as they tried to get a confession on the case. This would be a highly politicized case and the mayor's office would have its eye on the investigation. Rob sat and rocked in the straight back chair with a dead man stare focused at the ceiling.

"Praise Yahweh," said Rob over and over, and over, again, and again.

CHAPTER 11 - Investigations

Rob Ross was between a stone and a hard

spot. He was facing major time for the weapons

assault which included murder. Rob contemplated

his situation and concluded he had no choice but to

cooperate. The street code was clear and anyone

that rat faced the worst condemnation. However he

was looking at the possibility of life in jail or even

the death penalty. He would have to save his own

hide and reveal the inner workings of El Cid's

organization to the cops.

El Cid was uncertain how to react on the

news that his top enforcer was in the hands of the

authorities. El Cid was aware that Rob already had

a lengthy rap sheet and would obviously rat under

pressure. He would have to move decisively and

decided to hire a media savvy high-level attorney from West Palm Beach.

El Cid sat in the downtown office of Dale Cox and relayed the relationship he had with Rob in the movement. Dale's office was located in on the top floor of a downtown hi-rise and overlooked the intra-coastal harbor. Sailboats and yachts could be seen as they entered the waterways from their exotic trips to sea.

El Cid sat with his robes draped over the oak wood chair in Dale's office. Dale sat at his oversized Mahogany desk that was neatly stacked with papers. Dale was the only black attorney in the city that had not lost a case in the media. His Armani suits and Italian shoes more than complimented his commanding air with clients.

"What do you want to do about this situation minister," inquired Dale.

"I want to quash all the rumors surrounding my movement by inviting the media and my friends in politics to tour the compound," said El Cid.

He believed the tour would give outsiders a view of how his followers have accepted the faith. He was confident that his detractors in the community would be silenced upon seeing the cooperative work ethic of the Sufi nation.

***

In the meantime Rob was cooperating with the detectives and he was singing like a bird for his freedom. He revealed a time when dissenters were suspected of going to the police about pedophilia rumors against El Cid that were occurring in the compound. He spoke in detail of how they were silenced.

"I and two other brothers wore black ski masks and we attacked Yakim along with his wife at their home," he said.

"Why," Inquired a detective.

"El Cid got word that Yakim had gave a statement to police about him sleeping with their 12 year old daughter," he said.

"What happened," asked the detective.

"We shot Yakim to death and slit his wife's throat," said Rob in a detached tone.

His casual manner of describing the assault gave an impression of indifference and reflected the coldness of his heart. He had once been a star athlete admired and loved by many of his peers. He now was a devolved killer for El Cid and the Sufi nation with no regard for humanity. El Cid set out

to make walking zombies of his followers and he

didn't stop at just the ordinary parishioner. His

guards, henchmen, and soldiers were well

brainwashed in carrying out the edicts issued by

him. Law enforcement was slow to catch on to the

rising tide of violence surrounding the cult. They

now faced the whirlwind.

***

The compound was overhauled in

anticipation of the many visitations El Cid had

scheduled for the coming months. Walls were

painted, new furniture bought for residents and new

clothes for the distressed. It was as if Christmas

had come to the Sufi nation and El Cid put money

into revamping the attitudes of his flock. As

dignitaries such as commissioners, mayors, and

local pastors toured the facility they saw the layout

of communal living. The schools had immaculate

modern classrooms for children and adult learning.

The cafeteria was clean and well stocked with

fruits. The living areas consisted of wood furnished

condos with dwellings for family and single living.

The print shop was vibrant with workers processing

orders and the worship area was on display with its

ornate artwork.

The mayor of Miami along with other

officials was highly impressed with what they saw

of the facility. Word spread in the community of

the highly organized way of living in the

compound. Reporters quickly interviewed those

with knowledge of the inner operations of the

compound for more personal details of the lifestyle

there. Group living was always a phenomena and a remnant of the hippie movement of the sixties.

Plain-clothes police were also among the officials that toured the compound and they were vigilant of anything that raised criminal suspicions. They patrolled the warehouse facility full time with unmarked squad cars. They constantly sized up the turban wearing Magnificent Seven and kept them under tight surveillance. The seven went from brandishing long knife machetes to wearing large flashlights. They dwindled to roaming the compound in pairs of two to appear less menacing. El Cid was successful in displaying the Sufi movement as a sole business empowerment movement dedicated to the building of the community. Little did he know the wheels of justice were in motion.

***

Rob Ross sat in the investigation room at a small table with an empty coffee cup and a bag of salted peanuts in front of him. The room was without windows and he had no concept of time as he was interviewed for hours at a time by investigators. He was drained of energy and he sat hunched over in the wooden chair trying to get some degree of comfort from it. A detective came in and stood over him.

"Ok Ross let's hear more details of the murders," he inquired.

Rob looked up at the officer and strained to focus on his face. His vision was blurred and he struggled to keep his eyelids open. He thought to himself at this point he would do and say anything for a little rest. Rob knew at one point he would have to answer for his crimes but did not realize the

degree of mental brutality he would endure.

"Fine, just stop invading my personal

space," he replied.

The officer stepped away and pulled a chair

directly in front of Rob. Rob drummed through his

thoughts and strained to relax in the chair. The

detective sat alert in his chair and waited

impatiently for him to start talking.

"El Cid has a fascination with death and he

rewards the killing of any person that's white," he

said.

The detective who was white looked as if he

was appalled.

"What?" replied the cop.

"Individuals that commit murder upon whites are called death angels of El Cid and he rewards them for these deeds," said Rob.

"I would go out in the Coconut Grove area within the gay neighborhood and hunt for people to kill. Anyone weak or small would be easy prey for murder and I would do this alone," he said.

"There was once this drunk white gay man stumbling as he walked home from a gay bar and he caught my attention. I followed him and he was oblivious to my presence because he wasn't in his right frame of mind. As he opened the door to his apartment I barged in and began beating him up. I stabbed the man in his heart and killed him. The crazy thing about that kill was that the man had a roommate who was asleep on the couch. I had to kill him also because he witnessed the entire thing,"

he said.

The officer jotted something on a note pad

he had before continuing with the interview. As the

officer wrote his notes Rob sat with a blank

expression on his face and adjusted in the chair

stilling trying to comfort himself.

"That's a hard seat, huh," the officer

inquired.

"Yeah," replied Rob.

"Good," he countered.

"Anything else," the officer asked.

Rob wiggled in the chair a bit before

answering the officer's inquiry. He was tired and

wanted rest. He decided to give one last story

before requesting rest or complaining about his

current condition. He cleared his throat and began speaking in a lowered tone.

"El Cid was very suspicious of people and a new comer arrived at the camp saying he was from New Orleans. He was a very weird guy and he would do things like space out during prayer study. He would also get into fights with other parishioners which brought attention from the elders," said Rob.

As Rob spoke he could see he had the full attention of the detective and he felt compelled to include every detail he could remember of the incident. The incident had occurred years ago and he had place the memory in the back of his mind until now. It was good for him to compartmentalize things in order to complete any dastardly deed needed for El Cid.

"This one fight the guy was involved in El Cid interceded and asked the guy was he sent to assassinate him. There was a crowd of about forty people gathering to watch the disruption and the guy told El Cid he had come to be enlightened. El Cid was not moved by this reply and the mob attacked the guy. El Cid did nothing to stop them and the guy had his eyes gouged out and his groin mutilated," said Rob.

"What was the name of this guy," asked the officer.

"Mike Dupree," replied Rob.

"Guards locked the compound gates and no one was allowed to leave. El Cid made everyone present at the scene – man, elderly and children – hit this guy while he lay dying. He bonded these people to him in blood. No ones hands would be clean and no one could run to the cops," said Rob.

"What happened to the body," asked the detective.

"It was rolled up in an old piece of carpet and dumped in the canal," he replied.

The men in the office listened in horror and were disgusted at what they heard. The detective scribbled feverishly on his pad. The other officers looked away in disbelief and one officer dry heaved in a nearby garbage can. Rob lopped his head down as if he had just released a heavy weight from his neck. The detective was slow to disperse the occupants from the room because he knew the press was waiting. People milled the halls of the police station and many awaited the details of the confession.

CHAPTER 12 - Turn Coats

Rob's statements were beneficial to
investigators in securing an arrest warrant of El Cid
and his top brass. El Cid faced a 25-page
indictment on extortion; racketeering and 15
disciples were wanted on 14 murders. El Cid was
on travel and not in Miami when the media
announced the indictment. He attended the Feast of
the Tabernacle conference in New Orleans, and was
arrested while he traveled back to Miami.

The details of the indictment were made
public and many in the city were surprised at the
findings of the report. Reporters hounded local
politicians whom supported El Cid and the Sufi
movement. Public officials readily condemned El
Cid and admonished him as a con man peddling

religion. El Cid's followers were shocked upon

hearing of his arrest and dissenters began to desert

the compound by the hundreds. The guards and the

Magnificent Seven were powerless to stop them, as

they were concerned with being indicted

themselves.

The local residents of Liberty City were not

surprised of the findings of the indictment. They

had heard the stories for years and found the

reactions of the majority amusing when realization

of blatant abuse of power was uncovered in their

city. Officials babbled to reporters attempting to

rationalize the scandal and minimize their

associations.

El Cid sat in the Miami Dade County Jail

awaiting to be arraigned on the charges of the

indictment. He of course had already hired a high-powered attorney in anticipation of such an

occasion. His attorney quickly initiated an attempt

to have him released on bail under his own

recognizance.

In court El Cid stood along with his lawyer

in front of the judge to partition for his release. The

prosecuting attorney detailed the wealth of the Sufi

nation organization and released financial records of

El Cid's bank statement. El Cid's political

connections failed to empower him at this moment

and he was remanded to lockup with no bail

because of the flight risk he posed.

Elizabeth took over the day-to-day

operations of the movement as El Cid sat in jail and

fought with the legal proceedings of his case.

Elizabeth had the job of overseeing the financial

and administrative operations of the movement.

She was there from the beginning and had watched the movement blossom from nothing. Many of the followers saw her as El Cid's first lady of the movement. It was true that she had been with him from the start but she was not corrupted by the visages of power.

As Elizabeth sat in the office of the compound she poured over financial records to access the stability of the organization and its investments. Dale Cox entered the office unescorted because the militant structure of the movement had since diminished due to the arrests.

"I see everything has been left in good hands," said Dale.

"It's always been in good hands," replied Elizabeth.

"El Cid built this organization from nothing and now it is worth millions," said Dale. "What qualifies you to take over," he inquired.

Elizabeth had not looked up from what she was doing but now paused from leafing through a stack of folders centered on her desk. Dale stood with his hands in his suit pockets awaiting a response.

"I was here from the start and I'm still standing," she replied.

"I owe no one any explanations and I feel the only reason there's a concern is because I'm a woman," she said.

Elizabeth sat back in her chair and her mind was now running. She had been second in command for so long. She had handled administrative problems and financial improprieties.

She was no teacher or preacher but she ensured everything ran smoothly in the organizations and she got little accolade.

"Listen I have years of experience as a certified secretary and am graduate of Spelman College one of the top HBCU's in the nation. You will have no problem getting your money," she stated.

Dale chuckled lightly and fingered his car keys in his pockets. He glanced down to the floor and then up again at Elizabeth before he replied.

"Don't get yourself in a twist," he said. "I only wanted to know what I was dealing with."

He eyed a chair in the corner of the room and side stepped his way over to take a seat. The compound was quiet and the no one was in the office except for the two of them. He felt assured by the response he got in regards to his concern. He was unsure how stable El Cid's organization was and before becoming entangled legally set out to assess its finances. El Cid proved formidable as a leader and socialite. Nevertheless, Dale questioned the soundness of his financial escapades.

"It's likely the legal ramblings of the court will take a couple of years," he replied.

"And of course you want to ensure that El Cid will pay you," replied Elizabeth.

"No," said Dale. "I want to ensure I am paid."

"It's possible that the courts could freeze his assets and accuse him of fraud," said Dale.

"If that happens, all is lost."

***

The prosecutor set out to track down any and everyone that had a beef with El Cid. He wanted to obtain as much corroborating evidence against El Cid as possible. He did not want to get involved in the right to religion aspect of the case. His focus was on El Cid as an individual person guilty of manipulating others in accomplishing crimes. El Cid now lawyered up would prove a formidable task in court. One lady they tracked down would prove to be a real nail in the coffin for the case against El Cid. She had survived an attack where her husband was killed and the assailants attempted to slit her throat. Other dissidents were also volunteering their services to ensure El Cid's conviction.

The media had a field day with all of the sordid stories surrounding El Cid and the Sufi movement. The rumors of sex, murder, and

mayhem made headlines throughout the city and

garnered national attention. Reporters were paying

hundreds of dollars for exclusive interviews of cult

members and victims of El Cid. The newspapers

ran headlines painting El Cid as a homicidal

maniac.

The community was indifferent to the media

coverage of the Sufi movement and had known of

the stories of El Cid. The religious group was a

progressive movement in the black community and

had done much good despite the media coverage.

Some residents spoke highly of the programs

sponsored by the group. Some sided with El Cid

and believed he had rogue elements in his

organization. Some individuals believed that the

government in some type of Co-Intel- Pro trap, set
him up.

El Cid's attorney Dale Cox was becoming a
regular on the afternoon seven news and relentlessly
represented his client against all accusations. Dale
would make the prosecution work and fought all
judicial procedures for a speedy trial. It would take
the next twelve months before El Cid and his
cronies would stand before a judge and jury for the
allegations that faced them in court.

El Cid languished in the county jail because
his bail had been denied and his attorney was
powerless to get a release for him. The cell was
dirty and had a dingy mold smell to it. The cell bed
cots looked worn, smelled of urine and were
uncomfortable. They provided little leisure to the
man who ruled over a million-dollar enterprise.

• • •

El Cid was reduced to wearing prison garb. He initially tried to fight what he wore by claiming religious right. The jail officials were not impressed with his theatrics and he was forced to comply with jailhouse rules. His silk robes and jeweled head wraps would be reserved for court appearances only. Servants of the Sufi nation had once waited him on night and day. He was now reduced to menial work assignments for pennies on the dollar in the jail's furniture making factory.

Some of the other convicts were aware of El Cid's status as somewhat of a celebrity inmate and they did not cause problems for him. He was true to his nature and preached the word of his movement to captive audiences every chance he got. Supporters of the Sufi nation organized and supported El Cid with quiet protests for his release at any and all court proceedings. No matter the attention and good treatment he got, he could not adjust to being locked behind bars.

The isolation from his organization and the routine of jail life was vastly different from the opulent lifestyle he had developed for himself. The proverbial saying that absolute power corrupts absolutely was true in his case and he could not bring himself to feel regret for what had occurred.

He reasoned that he had not personally been involved and his hands were free of blood.

CHAPTER 13 - Locked Down

El Cid sat with his lawyer in the jailhouse conference room preparing for his trial date appearance. The room had no walls and no windows and was quite bare with the exception of a wooden table and two chairs that sat across from each other. There was a slight chill in the air as Florida jails kept the A/C running at all times.

"If there is anything you want me to know, you should tell me now," replied Dale Cox.

El Cid sat with his hands clasp together and his arms were outstretched over the length of the table. He eyed the attorney sternly before answering him. He repositioned himself in his chair and considered his predicament.

"Everything is out in the open," El Cid replied.

"Good let's get started," said Dale.

"The Key to your defense is to maintain your temper and just follow my advisement. You should have no problems," he remarked.

El Cid knew he had to remain calm and not get worked up over the events that were soon to be played out in court. The mascot of the court system is represented by a blindfolded image of a person balancing a scale. El Cid recognized the symbolism of this image and grudgingly respected it. From the talk of his fellow jail mates he knew the media was going to be massive in the coverage of the trial. Although he was going by another name he wondered if his old associates would get wind of his situation.

With the publicity of all his actions El Cid now faced open scrutiny for the sake of a conviction for the murders. His lawyer counseled him stating the facts of the case were principal and his life style had no influence on the case. This did not comfort El Cid and he had no trust in the government's justice system. He had no choice but to place his fate in the hands of the same system for which he harbored contempt.

El Cid's lawyer strongly advised him not to speak about his case while serving time in the county lockup. It was well known that inmates snitched on anyone that they could to get an early release date. In any high profile case snitches wait ready to obtain evidence on an inmate and relay to the DA or a cop for favors.

The lawyer departed and El Cid was led back to his cell on the 1st tier of the unit he was assigned. He sat behind bars and pondered his arrest which was a highly anticipated event by the media. He remembered being herded like an animal with the other inmates during processing, stripped and given five minutes to shower with a group of one hundred guys. They were provided with used towels to dry their bodies and he felt degraded.

The entire time of inmate processing took about 24 hours and this was an arduous process. The processors seemed overworked and uninterested in the concerns of the inmates. No food or water was given during this period and any one that had a medical condition possibly suffered horribly.

El Cid reclined on his bunk which was a

metal bed with a 2-inch foam mattress. Many

inmates throughout the years had probably used this

triple bunk. Other inmates lounged around him and

there was no expectation of privacy. He soaked up

the jail culture from the talks of his fellow inmates.

Blacks, Cubans, Whites and others were the

major sects that made up the jail population. Others

often consisted of Asians and other Hispanic non-

Cubans from other countries awaiting deportation.

El Cid found it strange that during times of

upheaval the whites banded with the blacks to

oppose Cubans. On the outside that's considered

Benedict Arnold like to either side.

El Cid's outlook on race was mainly with

concerns between black and white. He never

considered the other races relevant. In jail their

congregated numbers made them very relevant. If caught with no allegiance a person would have a very hard time making it behind bars.

One group that was very dangerous was the Columbians and they were violent against their fellow Cuban Hispanics. They were kept housed separate from the other inmates and received different recreational time orders. The Cubans hated the Mexicans and the Mexicans on occasion banded with the blacks in confrontations with Cuban mobs.

Every group had a shot caller and this was the head person that was the designated leader. El Cid was high profile and the leader for the blacks looked out for him. He was advised to not make friends and distrust all for his own protection. El

Cid was no fool and took the advisement with all the seriousness of a death sentence.

In pursuing his own religious practice he garnered a small following through his teachings. His only comfort was his worship and this gave him the drive to keep going on a daily basis. Most of the inmates gave El Cid no trouble and many were curious about his teachings. A few were astounded at the reputation of the Sufi nation and how El Cid had led his followers. The inmate mind state is one of control and power which rules their day-to-day living.

Comparable to inmates wolves have this mentality for better survival by living and hunting in packs. Packs are familial organized communities with a hierarchy of defined roles and a leader. This structure is reinforced by nips, fights and favors which drive the jail yard process.

***

The media headlines carried stories which admonished El Cid as a power struck leader of a successful mega church movement. Many of the political contacts El Cid had made tried frantically to disassociate themselves from him. They unfortunately were tied to him by monetary donations and other gifts they received over the years. The local businesses in the community owned by the Sufi nation were not adversely affected by the publicity. They remained open and were profitable. Elizabeth kept a tight control over all the business affairs of the organization as she feared the federal government was watching closely for improprieties.

She maintained many of the accounting records using the peach tree accounting system. This system of record keeping method was easy and efficient. It made the volume of records for the various businesses easy to manage. The business policies of the Sufi nation would not change but El Cid no longer had final say due to his legal predicament.

Elizabeth was leery in identifying trusted staff to help with the day-to-day management of business affairs. Many of the elders expressed concern, as she was a women stepping into a powerful role for the movement. They themselves did not have the background to lead in the way she did. She saw no reason in riding herself of them although they were in opposition of her role as leader of the business organization. She saw them as useful because of their roles as spiritual leaders.

She decided to use them but would be weary of

their advisement on any matters related to policy

decision making. She decided to hire a publicist to

handle all media matters related to the organization

and to rebuild the image of the movement.

Many of the insiders in the organization

were critical of the strategies Elizabeth sought to

implement. Some questioned the judgement of El

Cid in taking a woman into trusted confidence as he

did with Elizabeth. They dared not raise such

concerns directly to El Cid in fear of retribution.

Although the people squabbled among each other

and promulgated rumors they feared retribution.

CHAPTER 14 - Court

The Judge sat behind a huge raised oak desk in the downtown courtroom of Miami and it was said his bench was bullet proof. Years earlier a previous judge was killed as an innocent bystander when a cohort shot at a cocaine cowboy defendant. The Dade County legal system placed a lot of money in making security airtight during proceedings. The outside gallery was full cops and detectives as the hearings of El Cid and his associates begun. Behind the judge were colorful red and blue flags with tassels sprawled over their individual seals. Women holding scales, olive branches and doves adorned the flags and flagpoles. The traditions of rule of law and justice were the feelings evoked when looking upon such sites.

Beside the bench was a small uncomfortable

looking witness stand. There was also a stand for

the court clerk and court reporter for the

proceedings. The courtroom divided into two parts

and a brass railing separated the active participants

from the observing audience. A tall thick sized

bailiff stood against the wall ready to pounce on

anyone that attempted to disrupt the hearings. El

Cid could tell the man was prior military. He could

see part of a special units tattoo barely visible under

the rolled short sleeve of his uniform.

El Cid wondered if the man was in the Air

Force or the Army. His buzz cut gave him the look

of a Marine officer. El Cid had traveled a long way

from his days in the military and wondered had it all

led to this particular point in his life. He shuddered

as the cold courtroom air flowed through his robe

and tunic. Wearing his traditional garb for daily
court appearances made him feel a bit more at ease.

El Cid, his counsel, and the opposing
counsel sat across facing the judge. The jury box
was catty- corner from the judge's bench. The
courtroom appeared quite spacious with its high
ceilings and marble-diagramed floors. The entire
environment was constructed to appeal to the civic
aesthetic nature of governing in the City.

The Judge in his black robe banged the
gavel to start proceedings on the most violent case
heard in a federal court of South Florida as noted by
local newspapers. The prosecutor's initial attack
was on the savage nature of the killings blamed on
El Cid's followers. El Cid was described as a
vicious cult leader who demanded total loyalty by
way of murder. The Prosecutor recited the horrible

rumors that were rampant among followers living in the compound.

"Is it true that you exerted control over the men of your organization in conducting sex education class," inquired the lawyer.

"Objection," contended Dale. "There's no basis for this line of questioning."

"To the contrary judge, this reveals the state of mind of the defendant," stated the prosecutor.

"Proceed," replied the judge as he gave the prosecutor an inquisitive look.

El Cid looked out of place on the witness stand and his attire made him stand out among the men in dark suits. The courtroom was packed with people and all eyes were on him as the prosecuting attorney questioned him.

"In fact you personally conducted circumcisions on the males of your movement, correct," inquired the attorney.

"Yes," said El Cid.

"Are you a doctor or do you have a medical background, Mr. Miller?" The attorney asked.

"No," replied El Cid.

"Mr. Miller did you lead sex education classes for the women in your movement?" The attorney asked.

"Yes," replied El Cid.

"Your honor Mr. Miller exerted total control of his followers and in exchange for proving their loyalty they committed murder upon his solicitation," stated the attorney.

El Cid sat listening to the prosecutor make his case and he watched him gallivant around the courtroom as if he had a major revelation. His attorney Dale Cox entered El Cid's plea as not guilty and the connection the prosecutor was trying to establish was weak at best. It felt strange for El Cid to hear his government name in court. He had not heard that name in years and had since tried to kill it by adopting his current one. He had set out to build a legacy for self-sustainment and development for the ages. His background was a meager one and he had established a financial empire with his own ingenuity. He wondered why he was being attacked and blamed for the actions of others who acted on their own accord. It took hustle and grind to make it on the streets at whatever profession one took up. El Cid decided long ago that he would do whatever it took to eat and have a good life. He would not suffer at the hand of others if he could help it.

• • •

The prosecuting attorney took a seat and the preparation for the parade of witnesses was ready to take the stand. El Cid viewed these individuals as traitors and back bitters. He had provided sanctuary for these people and had given them purpose in life. They now sided with the oppressor and were trying to extinguish his life.

The judge banged the gavel and called for the first witness to take the stand. It was Rob Ross the former headman of the Magnificent Seven. He testified how the atmosphere within the movement was that of murder and mayhem towards so-called infidels. Rob admitted he killed people for the purpose of earning the favor of El Cid.

The dissenters of the Sufi nation filed into court and testified El Cid ruled the organization like a tyrant. El Cid maintained a poker face when the prosecutors showed jurors photos of victims who were savagely murdered by his followers. The prosecutors insisted that many people suffered in silence for fear of El Cid's inner circle.

"I saw my children starving," said one dissenter. "I was beaten by members of the M Seven and El Cid had sex with most of the women in the compound to include my wife."

Another witness testified that El Cid once remanded the compound's cafeteria to providing soup and bread in order to save money for the construction of an additional worship temple out of state. The witness went on to imply that El Cid starved families and children in the process. The jurors physically seemed moved by the testimony and El Cid's lawyer argued the relevance of the statement to the case at hand.

The reporters jotted notes and drew characterizations of all the witnesses which would be on the front pages of local newspapers the following day. The Sufi movement was receiving a lot of media attention and people were curious of the cult lifestyle. The cohorts on trail with El Cid received little attention, as El Cid was the major target of the prosecution.

Over one hundred people gave testimony in the case and the jury deliberated for two hours before bringing the verdict to the judge. The judge had recessed the court before the deliberations, was now settled with the proceedings and ready for the closing of the case. He was handed the verdict and reared back in his chair before making a statement.

"This has been the most violent case heard by the courts of Miami Dade County in decades and

may god have mercy on each of your souls," he
said.

The dissenters and the families of those
involved in the case waited with anticipation. Dale
Cox braced for the rest of the judge's remarks. He
knew that his case was high profile and believed it
would be a career changer depending on the verdict.

"Chauncey Miller AKA El Cid I sentence
you to 18 years in prison," he stated with a bang of
his gavel.

Each of El Cid's co-defendants got 15 years
in prison and the courtroom erupted in disbelief of
the verdict. El Cid at the age of 60 had risen from
obscurity to become one of the most powerful
African- American institutions in Miami. He would
be eligible for parole within ten years. The Bailiff

immediately stepped forward and escorted him in

preparation of his new home.

Thank you for reading RISEN and be sure to leave a review. Also check out other titles from Thomas Barr Jr. and more at www.Printhousebooks.com

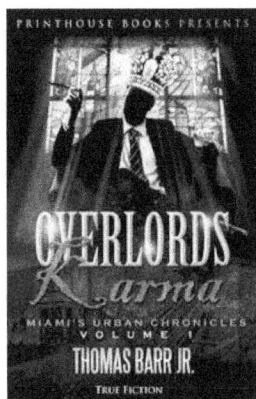

A policeman remembered the day of the death of Miami commissioner Amp Tate. Blood oozed over the marble floor of the most prominent news institution in Miami. Powerful commissioner Anthony "Amp" Tate laid stretched out with a gaping hole in his chest. With the gun still clutched in his hand, he attempted to speak to those gathered around him as he gasped his final breaths and died. Days before, Tate was indicted on corruption charges and profiled in Miami News as the City of Miami's most corrupt politician.

Tate, a towering 6 foot -5 inch tall African American, was the commissioner of the only black district in Miami. He previously held the position as chair of the commission and was current head of the Overtown Development Corporation, with additional duties of entertainment permitting. Tate a self-made man represented the interests and concerns of Miami's black community.

The policeman stationed in the lobby of the Miami News building rushed over when he heard the shot and screams. An elderly woman with her hands filled with a stack of papers fainted and littered the floor with her correspondences. The papers were soon matted with the commissioner's bright red blood as it leaked over the floor of the lobby. The cop stood over the commissioner uncertain what to do, as he had seen many fatal gunshot wounds of this sort.

This man has bought it, he thought to himself. People scattered sprinting for the lobby stairway and exit doors. He yelled for someone to call 9-1-1. The cop jumped back from the body being careful not to get blood on his shiny black boots. Blood spewed from the hole in the commissioner's back as the bullet had ripped clean thru his chest. The cop looked on in pity as the commissioner's body initiated a series of involuntary jerks from his stiffened limbs.

■■■

Two men initially in line ahead of the commissioner peered over the officer's shoulder at the body. "I wonder what he was trying to say," said one man looking down on the corpse.

• • •

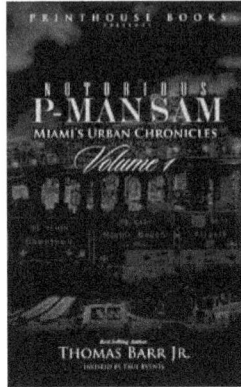

This book is about the struggle of African American men as they traverse the perils of 20th and twenty first century life in the professional realms of the work place atmosphere. The differences in opportunities are often overlooked in comparison to other classes and among the races.

The American dream is the realization of success in the face of struggle and hard work. Is it relevant that one's struggle is harder than the other in accomplishment of this goal? P-Man Sam is a hard look at the road to self-empowerment and

what it takes to make it in the American society.
The entrepreneurial spirit is one of the main roads
traveled in realization of the American dream.
It takes knowledge and a fearlessness to take a
chance in the ruthless world of business in this
society. It's also important to be able to effectively
communicate with the modern diverse society of
today through effective people skills.

The P-Man Sam story brings an awareness of how
to navigate negative experiences and transform
them into motivational learning blocks. Learning
from experiences and moving forward is essential
in life. One's eyes must be open and naïve thought
processes must be conquered in attaining the
ultimate prize. The following are useful for
application:

- Mentorship
- Net working
- Coalition building
- Broad-mindedness

This book is a good source for inspiration and having hope is a major force in your journey through life. Situations and circumstances should not be viewed as a hindrance, but instead a hurdle in step to the finish line. There are many instances in this story that relay the struggle against forces that present obstacles. Willpower and dedication are true factors that assist the main character in winning out against such forces.

In conclusion, the power of love and support are sustaining factors in the realization of goals in life. The act of goal-setting itself is an important factor in accomplishing anything in pursuant of ambitious dreams. This novel is sprinkled with kernels of knowledge and inspirational wording designed to give the reader insight into the motivations of the main character that can be transcending to experience.

It is beneficial and intended to identify and acquire these gems of knowledge to retain as progressive career tools.

Risen

PRINTHOUSE BOOKS

Read it, Enjoy it, Tell a friend.

VIP INK Publishing Group, Incorporated.

Atlanta, GA

www.ingramcontent.com/pod-product-compliance
Lightning Source LLC
Chambersburg PA
CBHW030830090426
42737CB00009B/953